BILL & GLORIA GAITHER

PRESENT

A Treasury For Kids

Gaither Music
COMPANY

A NOTE TO GROWN-UP KIDS
(Parents, Grandparents, Or Any Other Grown-Up)

We've tried very hard for a long time to tell children that they are a **PROMISE**. We want them to know that God puts a high value on the human person...so high that He even gave His Son for us. But the opinion that matters most to your children is yours, because they love you most! What you say will represent God to them; that's a heavy responsibility — but it is also one of life's greatest joys!

Remember this **INCREDIBLE** fact...God **CARES** about you. You are very special, too.

Bill Glass

FROM THE INSIDE OUT

words by Kathie Hill
and Janet McMahan

music by Kathie Hill
and Janet McMahan

Moderately fast 4

KIDS:

La,_____ la, la, la,_____ la, la, la,_____ la, la, la._____ 1. When
(2.Now if)

VERSE

I look in the mir - ror, I see my bod-y and my face and my
(2) God took an in - ven-tor - y, I'll tell you what He'd

4

hair; And I have to con-fess that I'm of - ten a mess, And I
check: He'd wan-na make sure that your heart was pure - That's the

don't like what I see there!__ But when God is look - in' at__
first place He'd in - spect!__ And if He found that you loved Je -

ADULT:(both times)

__ me He knows just where to start:
- sus with your heart and soul and might, Then

ALL(2nd time only)

He looks deep in - to my heart.
He'd say you checked out al - right! From the in - side__ out

tacet

CHORUS

God's look-in' at me;

(From the in - side_ out)

(God's look-in' at me;)

From the in - side_ out

I hope He likes what He sees!

(From the in - side_ out)

ALL:

(I hope He likes what He sees!)

From the out - side I might not

look so good, But you might change your mind if you on-ly could_

*Kids sing cue notes ("Echo") on first chorus, then switch parts on second chorus.

1.
Bb7
Eb
KIDS:
See me from the in - side out! La, la, la, la,
Bb
Ab
Bb
D.S. to verse 2
mp
la, la, la, la, la, la.
2. Now if
2.
Bb7
Gm/Bb
See me from the in - side, see me from the in - side,
Eb unis.
See me from the in, in - side out!
8va

God CAN

Words and Music by Mrs. Lee Roy Abernathy

Intro

I can't tell when friends are true, but
I can't make a sim-ple cloud, but God can.
I can't calm a rag-ing sea, but

I can't look in-side of you, but
I can't feed a hun-gry crowd, but
Can't make hon-ey like a bee, but

God can.
Can't turn dark-ness in-to light, can't make moun-tains snow-y white,
I can't make the lame to walk, I can't make the dumb to talk,
I can't make the light-ning stop, can't make earth pro-duce a crop,

Bb7

can't give blind – ed eyes their sight, but God
can't put corn up – on a stalk, but
I can't make it rain a drop, but

Eb **Bb7**

can. (1 & 2)Some-times I won - der in His plan if
3. Our great men show their might-y pow'r on

Eb **F7**

He in - clud - ed me, And then I think how one small a - corn
land, in air, on sea; But sci - ence can't pro - duce one thing that

3rd time to ⊕

Bb **Bb°** **Bb7** **Eb** **Eb7** **Ab** **Fm**

makes the big oak tree.
lives or dies or breathes.

1. I can't make the morn - ing dew, I can't make the skies of blue,
2. God will give the strength we lack; fol - low on and don't look back,
3. I don't know just what's in store, I can't see thro' Heav-en's door,

I can't make a dream come true, but God can;
some-times we can't see the track, but God can.

CODA

nev-er walked this way be-fore, don't know what we're ask-ing for, I can't tell you an-y-more, but

God can. *(spoken)* but God can!

GOD LOVES TO TALK TO Little BOYS (WHILE THEY'RE FISHIN')

Words by
WILLIAM J. and GLORIA GAITHER

Music by
WILLIAM J. GAITHER

GEORGE: Have you ever heard God talkin'? He does you know? To us!
But most of the time we're just not list'nin'!

Gently ♩ = ca. 66

Adult Male Solo (freely)

on - ly qui - et time there is for wish - in', ___ it's the

A

B7

on - ly time when God and boys can rest.

E7

A

F7

MADISON:
You know, a boy, a boy can almost hear God whisper sometimes out here fishin'. I wonder if He's

B♭

C7

just tryin' to tell me somethin'? Excuse me just a minute, Mr. George, while I just sit here and listen for a spell.

F7

B♭

B♭7 Cm B♭7/D

12

GEORGE: You go right ahead, Madison, you go right ahead, son!

God loves to talk to lit-tle boys while they're fish-in', that seems to be the time boys lis-ten best. There's

some - thin' ___ 'bout a boy who's good at fish - in', ___ God

Bb   C7

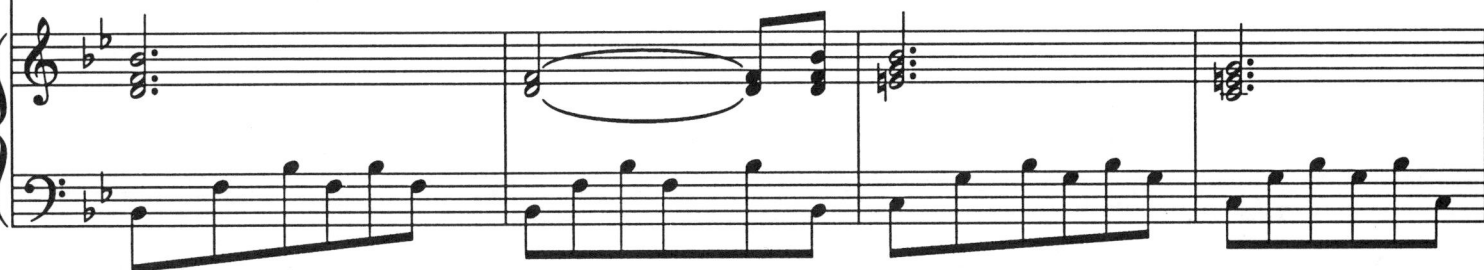

knows he'll make a ver - y spe - cial friend.   A

F7   Bb   Bb7   Cm   Bb7/D

boy who learns to lis - ten while he's fish - in' ___ can

Eb   Bb   G7

hear God when it's time to fish for men.   God

C9   F7   F#7   G#m   F#7/A#

61

loves to talk to boys while they're fish - in', ___ that

B   C#7

seems to be the time boys lis - ten best. It's the

F#   C#m/F#   F#   B   E/F#

69

on - ly qui - et time there is for wish - in', ___ it's the

B   C#7

molto rit.

on - ly time when God and boys can rest.

MADISON: Mr. George, I'm glad we went fishin' today.
GEORGE: Me too, Madison, me too!

F#13   F#7   B   Bmaj7   E/F#   B

molto rit.   *freely*

I AM A PROMISE

Words by William J. and Gloria Gaither

Music by William J. Gaither

I am a prom- ise, I am a

pos- si- bil- i- ty, ___ I am a prom- ise ___ with a cap- i- tal "P" ___ I am a

great big bun- dle of po- tent- i- al- i- ty. ___

A / **D** / **Am7** **D**
And I am learn-in' _____ to hear God's voice _____ and I am

G / **G#dim.** / **D/A** / **B7aug.** **B7**
try-in' _____ to make the right choic - es, I'm a prom-ise to be _____

E7 / **G/A** / **D** **D/F#** / **Em7** **A7** **D**
an - y - thing God wants me to be. _____ I can

D / **Eb** / **E**
go an - y - where that He wants me to go, _____ I can be an - y - thing that He

(building gradually)

wants me to be, __ I can climb the high moun-tains, I can cross the wide sea, I'm a

great big prom - ise, you see! I am a prom - ise, I am a

pos - si - bil - i - ty, __ I am a prom - ise __ with a cap - i - tal "P", I'm a

great big bun - dle of po - tent - i - al - i - ty. __

18

I Choose TO BE YOUR CHILD

words by Gloria Gaither

music by William J. Gaither

Slowly, gentle feel

KIDS:(2nd and 3rd times only)

(2,3. I'll fol - low)

(2nd and 3rd times *only*)

You ev -'ry day when I can't see my

ADULT: (1st and 3rd times *only*)

(1,3.) Lord, I choose to be Your

D G D/F# G/D D
way - I know that I can
child - I place my trust in
E9 A7 D
trust You; I'll climb the hills, sail the
You; I will
G/D E7 A7
seas take me an - y - where You please -
fol - low all the while -

G
D/F♯
G/D
D
Em7/B
A7
Je - sus, You know how I love
Je - sus, You know how I love
1,2.
D.S. twice
3.
D
KIDS:
D
G
You. I'll fol - low You. Je - sus, You
You.
1,2.
D.S. twice
3.
D
Em7/B
A7
D
know how I love You.

I JUST GOTTA TELL Ya!

words by Gloria Gaither

music by William J. Gaither
and Jeff Kennedy

Easy 2, very syncopated!

KIDS:

VERSE

1. Well, I just___ got - ta tell___ ya what's
(2. I just)___ got - ta tell___ ya - you'll

hap - pen - in'___ to me___ 'Cause try - in' to keep
see I'm not___ the same___ Since my old dis - po -

still is an im-pos-si-bil-i-ty!___ All that
si-tion Je-sus trad-ed for His name!___ *A

time they tried to show___ me, But now you would-n't know___
New Life was His pres-ent, (And now I'm down-right pleas-

___me: I'm chang -
-ant!)

in'! I just got-ta tell___

* One second verse, one boy may sing: "A New Life was His present," while another child answers:
("And now he's down right pleasant"!)

A
C♯
ya what's hap - pen - in' to me I
Am
C
B7sus
B7
just can't keep a sec - ret and I've got - ta make you see!
Em
I just got - ta tell ya, I
F♯7sus
F♯7
Bm
just got - ta tell ya; I just got - ta tell

E7sus   **E7**

ya- Hey, I just got-ta tell— ya what's been

Em7   **F♯m7**   **G**   **G/A**   **A**

hap - pen - in'_____ to____

D   **C**   **G/A**   ADULT **Dsus/A**

me! If

F♯m7   **Bm7**   **Em7**

you could see in - side of me,— you'd be ex - cit - ed, too;—

What I dreamed_ that I could be_ is
start-in' to come true;_ There_ has been a ren-o-va-
-tion, an awe-some trans-for-ma-tion- I
just can't keep my-self from tell-ing you!_

D.S. al coda
I just
D.S. al coda
CODA
D
G
D
D
C
D
D
Just got - ta tell ya!
CODA
C
D
D
Db
Eb
Eb
Just got - ta tell ya! Well, I just got - ta tell
Db
Eb
Eb
f
ya, I just got - ta tell ya! Well, I

just got - ta tell__ ya what Je - sus did for me:__

He changed my mood, my at - ti - tude's__ im -

prov - ing, you will see! __ I just got - ta tell__

__ ya, I just got - ta tell__ ya, I

29

just got - ta tell ya, and I'd sure'd like to sell

ya on what Je - sus

did for me!

I EXPECT A MIRACLE

words by Gloria Gaither
and Reba Rambo

music by William J. Gaither
and Dony McGuire

Bright, with "anticipation"!

ADULTS:
(1st time only) CHORUS

I an-tic-i-pate__ the in-ev-it-a-ble,

su-per-nat-ur-al in-ter-ven-tion of God:__ I ex-pect a

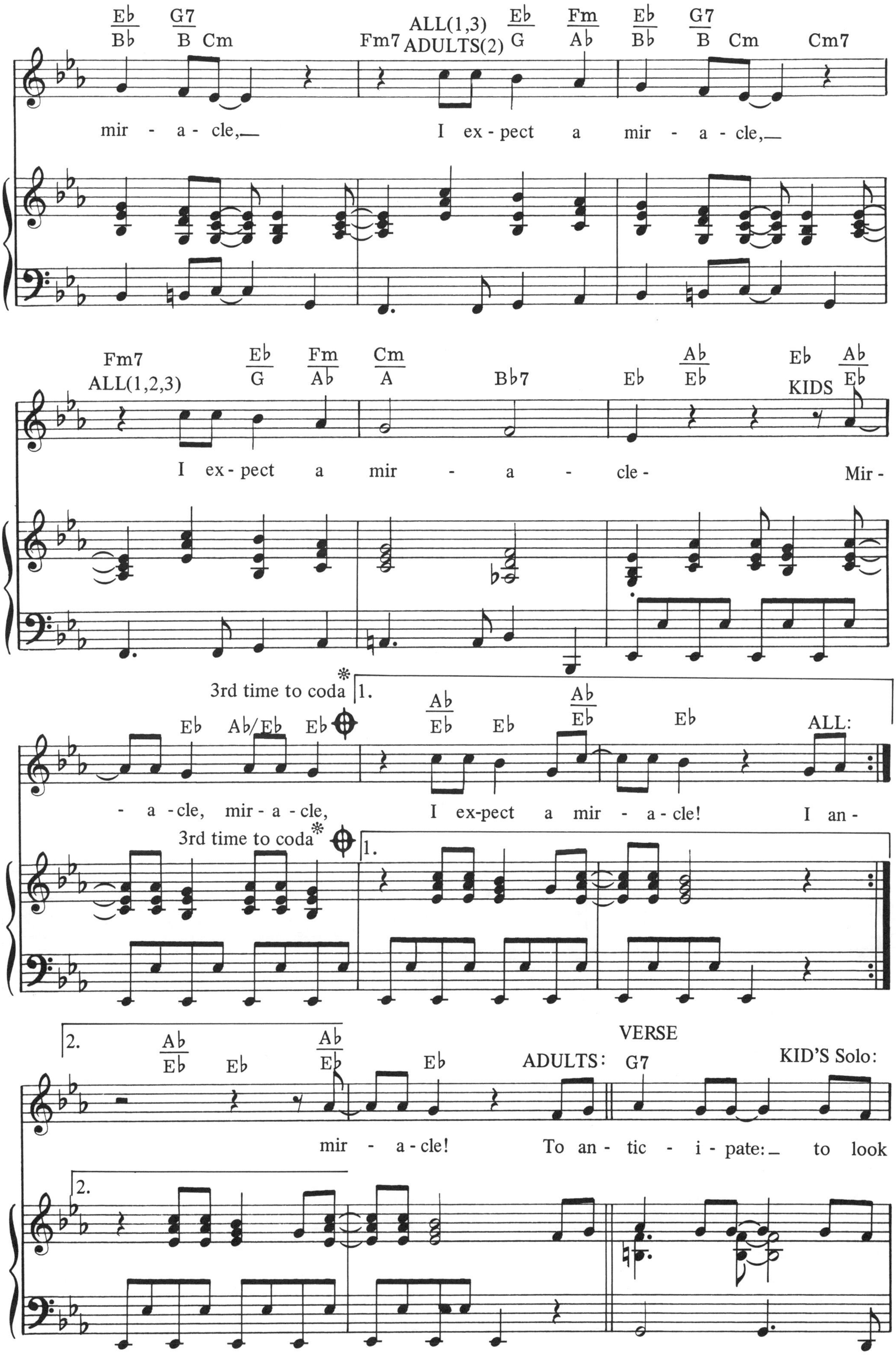

*Coda is *optional!* (You may choose to repeat chorus and fade.)

for - ward to___ what is like - ly to oc - cur;___

ADULT Solo: In - ev - it - a - ble:___ KID'S Solo: that cer - tain

some - thing bound to hap - pen. ADULTS: Su - per -

nat - ur - al:___ the pow'r be - yond___ all na - ture and___ di - vine___

KIDS:
F7sus
Whose in - ter - ven - tion comes be - tween
F7
me and my
Ab/Bb
prob - lems
ALL:
Ab/Bb
just in time!
(ALL) D.S.
I an -
D.S.
Coda
ALL:
Ab/Eb
Eb
Ab/Eb
Eb
I ex - pect a mir - a - cle!
Coda

I WONDER HOW IT FELT

Words by William J. and Gloria Gaither

Music by William J. Gaither
Arr. by Donna Huff

Intro

1. I won-der how it felt___ to
won-der how it felt___ to

wake up in the bel-ly of a whale,_____ I won-der how it felt___ to
meet big Go-li-ath in the field,_____ I won-der how it felt___ to

spend the night with Si-las in the jail;
know the mouth of li-ons had been sealed;

I'm just a child,_ my life is still be-fore me,__ I just can't wait__ to
I'm just a child,_ my life is still be-fore me,__ I just can't wait__ to

see what God has for me, but I know that I will trust Him and I'll wait and see what life will be for
see what God has for me, but I know that I will trust Him and I'll wait and see what life will be for

1.

me.   2. I

2.

To Next Strain

me.   3. I

won - der how it'd be_____ to watch your ba - by bro - ther in the nile, I won-der who would come,__ a

prin-cess or an an-gry cro-co-dile;

I'm just a child,__ my life is still be-fore me,__ I just can't wait__ to

see what God has for me, but I know that I will trust Him and I'll wait and see what life will be for me.

I'm just a child,__ my life is still be-fore me,__ I just can't wait__ to

see what God has for me, but I know that I will trust Him and I'll

wait and see what life will be for me._____

I'M SOMEBODY

words by Gloria Gaither

music by William J. Gaither
and Chris Christian

I'm some - bod - y, *(I'm some- bod -y) I said, "some-

bod- y;" (I said, "some- bod- y") I'm cre - a - ted in the im- age of

*Cue notes - 1st time only

Cmaj7
G
C
G
CHILD:
C6
G7
ADULT:
God, and I'm some - bod - y. (I'm some - bod - y) You're some -
(I'm)
C6
C
G
CHILD:
C6
C♯°
ADULT:
Dm7
CHILD:
bod - y, (I'm some - bod - y) yes, you're some - bod - y; (yes, I'm some -
(I'm)
G7
ADULT:
Dm7
F
G
G7
bod - y) You are loved and you're His child you're im - por - tant to
I am loved and I'm His child I'm im - por - tant to
C
D
E
E7
A
Him. (ADULT) 1. Nev - er be a - shamed if
Him. (CHILD) 2. I'll start each day

Amaj7
Bm7
you're not the same as the oth - ers,
What
hap-py just to say that I'm liv - in';
E9
E7
A2
A
you're meant to be is the ver - y best thing by far;
Think of all I have, thank-ful for the air that I breathe
Bm7
E7
A
Amaj7
You're a spe - cial plan cut from an o - rig - i - nal
I'll be sat - is - fied with the spe - cial gifts I've been
Bm7
1.
B7
pat - tern-
Just hold your head high, and re -
giv - en,
For
1.

mem-ber just Whose child you are!_____ I'm some -

God made no mis - take when He made me!_____ I'm some -

bod- y,____ *(I'm some-bod-y)* I said, "some-bod-y;"____ *(I said, "some-bod-y")* I'm cre -

a - ted in the im- age of God, and I'm some- bod-y.____ I'm some -

42

bod- y,___ *(I'm some-bod-y)* yes, I'm some-bod-y;___ *(I said, "some-bod-y")* I am

loved and I am His child I'm im-por-tant to Him!___

ADULT: Don't let anyone think little of you because you are young. Be their ideal ...be a pattern for them in you love, your faith and your clean thoughts!

(I Tim. 4:12, TLB)

We're some-

bod- y,___ we're all some - bod-y;___ We're cre -

*Optional!

Verses marked TLB all taken from The Living Bible, copyright 1971 By Tyndale House Publishers, Wheaton, Il. Used by permission.

Ebm7 Ab9sus Ab7 Db Dbmaj7/Ab Ebm7 Ab7
a - ted in the im - age of God and we're some-bod-y. We're some -
Db2 Db/Ab Dbmaj7 D° Ebm7 Ab7
bod - y, yes, we're some- bod - y; We are
Ebm7 Gb/Ab Ab7 Db6 Db/Ab 1. Db6 Db
loved and we're His chil- dren: im - por-tant to Him! We are
1.
2. Db6 Db Ebm7 Gb/Ab FmEbm/Ab Db
2.
rit.

IT'S A MIRACLE

Words by William J. and Gloria Gaither

Music by William J. Gaither

Bouncy (♩. =72)

1. What drives the stars with-out mak-ing a sound?
2. Who shows the birds how to make a good nest?

Why don't they crash when they're spin-ning a - round? What holds me up when the
How can the geese fly so far with-out rest? Why do the ducks go

world's up-side down? I know_____ it's a mir-a-cle._____
south and not west? I know_____ it's a mir-a-cle.

C   Cmaj7   C6   C   Dm   Dm7/C

Who tells the o-ceans where to stop on the sand? What keeps the wa-ter back from
What makes a brown seed so__ ti - ny and dry? Burst in - to green, _____

G7/B   G7   C   C7   F   Fm6

drown-ing the land?_____ Who makes the rules?__ I don't un - der - stand. I
grow up so high and shoot____ out blos-soms of red by and by? I

C/G   G7   C   C7   F   G9

know_____ it's a mir-a-cle!_____ It's a mir-a-cle_____
know_____ it's a mir-a-cle!_____

Em7   Am7   Dm7   G7   C   C7

just to know God is with me wher - ev - er I go. It's a

F	G9	Em7	Am7	D7(sus)	D7

mir-a-cle_____ as big as can be, That He can make a mir-a-cle of

1. G7	2. G7	Ab7

me.　　　me,　　A mir-a-cle of me. (3.) When a

Db	Dbmaj7	Db6	Db	Ebm	Ebm7 / Db

spring makes a brook and a **brook makes a stream,** The stream makes the riv-er wa-ter

Ab7 / C	Ab7	Db	Db7	Gb	Gbm6

fresh as can be.　　Who puts the salt in when it gets to the sea? I

D♭ B♭m7 E♭m7 A♭7 D♭ D♭maj7
know it's a mir-a-cle. There are thou-sands of peo-ple in
D♭6 D♭ E♭m E♭m7/D♭ A♭7/C A♭7
rit.
(Opt. spoken)
cit-ies I see, The world must be crow-ed as crowd-ed can be; But
rit.
D♭ D♭7 G♭ G♭m6
God knows my name and He cares a - bout me! I
a tempo
D♭ B♭m
know, I
a tempo

48

IT'S incredible!

Words by Gloria Gaither

Music by William J. Gaither

Moderate and rhythmic

It's in - cred-i-ble! It's in - cre-di-ble!

It's in - cre-di-ble! It's in-

cre - di - ble! Oh, it's in -

50

F9
E7 #9 b9
Am7/D
mf
Re - mem - ber
mf l.h.
B
G6
A7
God took a rough and tum - ble guy___ who liked to camp out in the wild;___
C/D
___ And He made him be the great an - noun - cer of the
G6
Ho - ly Mes - si - ah child.___ He took a sim - ple,___ trust - ing

52

God took a loud mouth fish-er-man, __ and a cow-ard *(spoken)* and a

cheat! And made them hon-est, kind and dar-ing men __ who could

stand up un-der heat. __ And God took a kid who

had two fish-es, and just five chunks of bread, __ And be-

54

cause that kid was so will-ing to share,___ an in-

cre-di-ble num-ber was fed!___ But more in-

cre-di-ble! God cares a-bout you and me,___ in-

cre-di-ble! Par-tic-u-lar-ly,___ be-cause in-

C
G
cre - di - bly! what we could turn out to be___ is in-
D
1.
G
D/A
G7/B
2.
G
E7♯9
cre-di-ble be-cause of His love! Oh it's in- love!
Am7
D7
G7
E7♯9
Am7
D7
(Repeat and fade)
be-cause of His love! be-cause of His

input/OUTPUT (THE COMPUTER SONG)

words by Kathie Hill

music by Kathie Hill
and Gary McSpadden

Strict 4 . . . "computer like"!

CHORUS

IN - PUT, OUT - PUT -

what goes in is what comes out,) IN - PUT, OUT - PUT -

B♭
that is what it's all a - bout; IN - PUT, OUT - PUT - your
F7
mind is a com - pu - ter whose IN - PUT, OUT - PUT
2nd time to coda
VERSE
B♭
F7
dai - ly you must choose.
1. Let the Bi - ble be your
2. If your print - out reads
2nd time to coda
B♭
F7
pri - mar - y feed - It's got all the
to lie or cheat, There's some da - ta

Bb   F7

da - ta you need;   Talk   to Je - sus
you should de - lete; De - bug   your mind of

Bb   C7

all   the time - That's the way   that you   can
sin - ful bytes- Then___ you   will op - e -

F   Gm7 / F   F7   Repeat twice to chorus

stay   on   line!
rate   all   right!

Repeat twice to chorus

CODA Bb   F7   Bb

IN - PUT,   OUT - PUT!

CODA

INTO MY HEART

Words and Music by Harry D. Clarke

In - to my heart, in - to my heart, come in - to my heart, Lord Je - sus! Come

G   D/F#   Em   D

in to - day,   come in to stay;   come

G   Bm/F#   Em 7   A7   D

in - to my heart,   Lord Je - sus!

Rubato

D   Gmaj7   F#m 7   Bm 7

Narration: That "happy" that happened at my house today-I thank You for making it happen that way.

Em 7   A7   G   Dsus2   D

I hope You'll forgive me the wrong things I've done: please know
that I didn't mean to hurt anyone.

I pray for the children all over the world;

give Your special care to each boy, and each girl. I thank You for loving and giving Yourself;

now please, help me share
You with everyone else!

Lord Je - sus! Come

in to - day, come in to stay; come

in - to my heart, Lord Je - sus!

JESUS, I HEARD YOU HAD A Big HOUSE

Words by William J. and Gloria Gaither

Music by William J. Gaither

($\quad$ = 60)

Simply, with feeling (Maintain triplet feel throughout - ♪♪ = ♪♪ *)* 1. Je - sus, I heard You had a

big house where I'd have a room of my own, And

Je - sus, I heard You had a big yard, big e - nough to let a kid

roam. I heard you had clothes in your clos - et

G   F#7 sus.   F#7   B7

just the right size that I wear,   and Je - sus, I heard if I'd

E9   G/A   A7   D   G   D/A   Em7 A7

give You my heart that You would let me go there.

D   Em7 F dim. D/A   D7   G   D

2. Je - sus, I heard a - bout meal - time when all of Your chil-dren come to eat.   I

D   Em7 F dim. D/A   B7   E9

heard You've got a great big ta - ble where ev - 'ry kid can have ___ a seat.   Je-sus, I heard there'd be plen - ty   of good things for chil-dren to

share,   And Je-sus, I just want to tell   You   I sure would like to go

there.   3. Je-sus, I heard that in your big   house there's

plen - ty of love to go 'round;   I heard there's al - ways sing-ing and laugh - ter to fill the place with hap - py sounds. And

I've been think-ing that a friend who'd planned to give me all that He's

got be-fore I had e -ven met Him, Well, He sure must love me a

lot! Yes, He sure must love me a lot!

Kids UNDER CONSTRUCTION

Words by Gloria Gaither and Gary S. Paxton

Music by William J. Gaither and
Gary S. Paxton

Bright 3

Kids un - der con - struc - tion —

may - be the paint is still wet!

Kids un - der con - struc - tion — the

C7

Last time to Coda ⊕   F

C   G7/D   C7/E

Lord might not be fin - ished yet.
(most have - n't turned___ out yet.)

1) I'm
2) Now
3) I
4) Dear

Verse

F   F/A   B♭   G7

more than an ac - ci - dent with - out a cause; I'm
mis - ter, I know that I get in your way; I'm
try to re - mem - ber the man - ners I've learned: My
Je - sus, please make us more pa - tient and kind—

C7   F   C   G7/D   C7/E

more than a bo - dy and brain. God
nois - y and just bug you so! But
"yes ma'am's" and "thank you's" and "please;" But
Help us to be more like You, And

F   F/A   B♭   G7   C7

made me on pur - pose — I'm part of a plan; He cares, and He
there's lots of ques - tions I just have to ask If ev - er I'm
I guess you think that more of - ten than not, I hol - ler and
make room for all oth - er chil - dren of Yours, For they are still

optional lyrics

Optional Verses

I drip on the carpet the snow from my boots,
And leave my coat on the chair;
But only this morning I made my own bed,
Got dressed and then brushed my own hair.

(Parent)

When you want to talk, I am watching the news;
Too often I ask "will it wait?"
Please keep interrupting, don't let me forget
That "later, son" may be too late.

The growing I do and what I become
Begins with the path that I take.
Now what I will be as I'm growing along
Depends on the choices I make.

Sometimes I'm discouraged with progress I've made—
It seems I've barely begun.
But when I look backward, I see where I've been;
I see all the growing I've done.

When I came to Jesus, I meant what I said—
I promised to give Him my heart.
But that kind of promise is more than just words;
Beginning was only a start.

All I can bring is all that I have,
All and no more or no less.
But all that I have is all God demands;
God mostly needs me to say "yes".

In the job of construction, I'm not all alone;
The Builder is working with me.
He's given the blueprint, the tools and the plan
To build all He wants me to be.

LET ALL THE Little CHILDREN PRAISE THE LORD

Words by William J. and Gloria Gaither

Music by William J. Gaither
Arr. by Donna Huff

Easy Swing (♩ =104)

Let all the lit-tle chil – dren__

praise the Lord,____ Let all the lit-tle chil - dren__
clap their hands,__

praise the Lord,_____ Let all the lit-tle
clap their hands,____

70

Let all the lit-tle chil-dren___ sing this song,_____ Let all the lit-tle chil-dren___ sing___this song,_____ Lit-tle chil-dren love to sing this song.___

L·I·F·e

words by Gloria Gaither

music by William J. Gaither

Easy, but rhythmic ("happy" sound)

VERSE

(ADULT)1.Gig - gles and tears____ and joy and sur - prise,____
(ADULT)2.Swim - ming and splash - ing - so warm in the sun,____

A♭6
Laugh - ter that's shin - ing in some - bod - y's eyes,
Build - ing a snow - man, a fire when we're done,
E♭9
ALL:
Work - ing and rest - ing, chuck - les and sighs:
Test - ing hot choc - 'late with hot - dogs and buns:
It
E♭
feels so good to be liv - in'!
E♭9
KID'S SOLO:
Burst - ing with se - crets when it's Christ - mas - time,
Watch - ing the spring - time ex - plode in - to bloom,

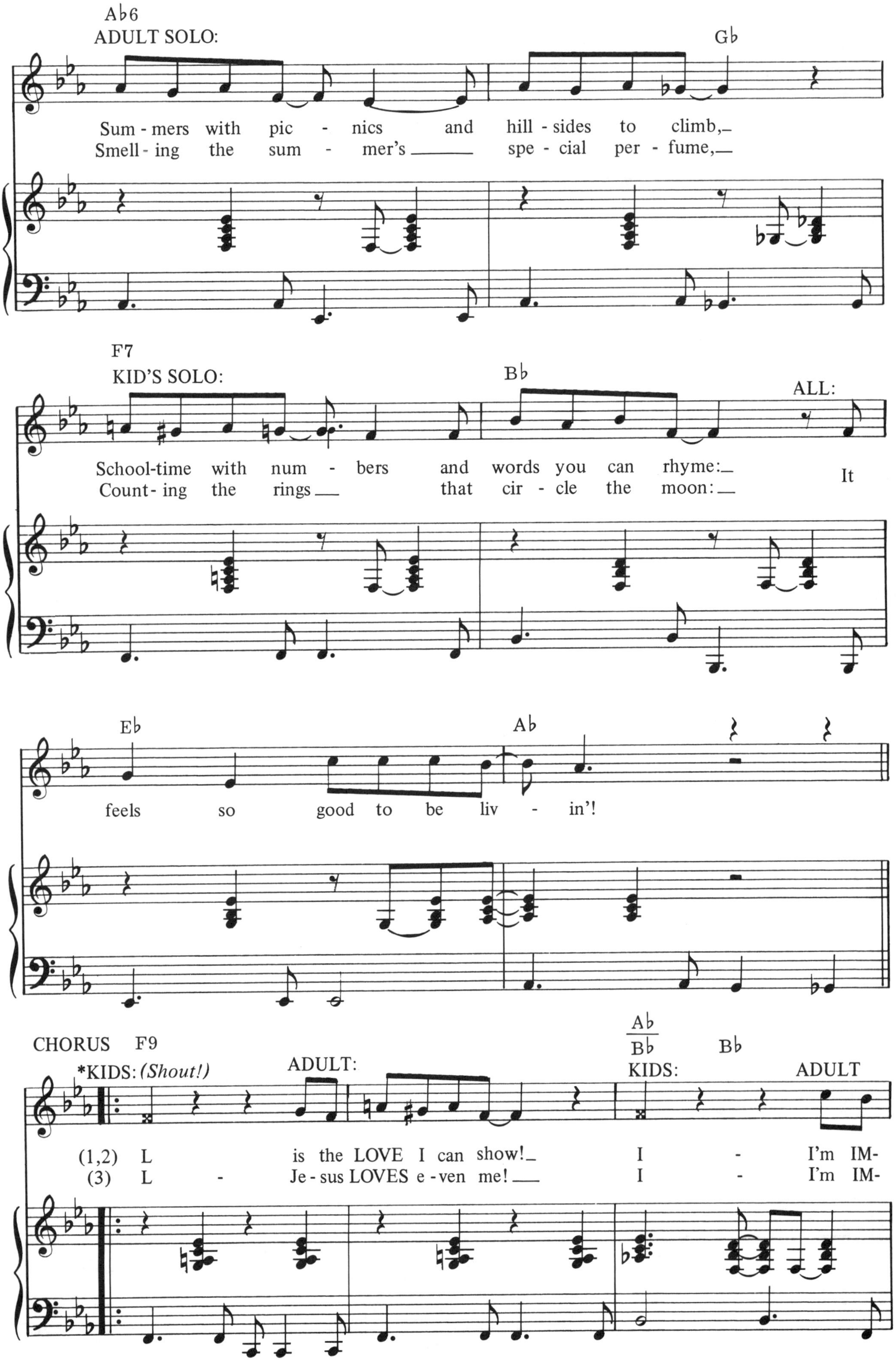

*On second chorus, kids and adults may switch parts.

Eb9
KIDS: ADULT:

PA-TIENT to grow!__   F -   that's the FRIENDS that I   know!__
POR-TANT, you see!__   F -   life's a   gift and it's   FREE!__

1. Db/Ab   Ab   Ab7(no 3rd)   Db/Ab   Ab   F9

ALL:

E means life's EX-CIT-ING and I just can't wait to go!

1.

mp

Eb7   Db/Ab   Ab   Absus   D.S. to verse 2

D.S. to verse 2

2. Db/Ab   Ab   G   Gb
     repeat to CHORUS

E means EV - ER - LAST - ING for   it   lasts   e - ter - nal - ly!

2.   *repeat to CHORUS*

E means EV - ER - LAST - ING for it lasts e - ter - nal - ly!

*ADULT: *Isn't it great to be alive?* KIDS: *Yeah!* ADULT: *Alright, give me an "L"!* KIDS: *"L"!!*

ADULT: *Give me an "I"!* KIDS: *"I"!!* ADULT: *Give me an "F"!* KIDS: *"F"!!*

ADULT: *Give me an "E"!* KIDS: *"E"!!* ADULT: *What does it spell?* KIDS: *LIFE!* ADULT: *I can't hear you!* KIDS: *(louder) LIFE!!*

(ad lib shouts and fade)

*This *spoken* ending is optional. If used, it should be definitely be spontaneous, enthusiastic and rather loud!! (Listen to Gloria and the kids on the recording.)

Love NEVER GIVES UP

words by Gary S. Paxton
and Gloria Gaither

music by Gary S. Paxton

Bright and happy, easy 4

CHORUS

ALL:

Love nev-er gives up, love

nev-er lets down; Love keeps on try - ing thru smiles or frowns. Love

Eb   Ab   Bb7   3rd time to coda ⊕

nev-er says die   e-ven when it gets   rough: True   love   just   nev-er gives

                                                                       3rd time to coda ⊕

1. | Eb / Eb6/Bb   Ebmaj7   Eb6/Bb   Eb   Eb6/Bb

up!

1.

Ebmaj7   Eb6/Bb   VERSE
                          ADULT: *mp* Eb   F7

                          1. No mat-ter what___ Je-sus loves you—   His

                                        mp

Fm7   Bb   Eb   Bb9sus   KIDS:

love   just keeps_go-ing   on   and on   and   on and on and on!   When oth - er friends__ dis -ap - point you, You can be sure__ He is

there all a - long!_____ 'Cause love up!

*SPOKEN: Love is very patient and kind...never jealous or envious...never boastful or proud...never haughty or

* This spoken part works well using several different voices... of all ages! (Listen to the record.)

selfish or rude. Love does not demand its own way. It is not irritable or touchy. It does not hold grudges

and will hardly even notice when others do it wrong.* (I Cor. 13:4-5, TLB)

VERSE

*Verses marked TLB are taken from The Living Bible, copyright 1971 By Tyndale House Publishers, Wheaton, IL. Used by permission.

ADULT: E♭   F7   KIDS:

more and more and more! It shares with-out_ hes - i - ta - tion, And

Fm7   B♭9sus   D.S. al Coda
ALL: mf

does-n't e - ven try to keep score,_ to keep score!_____ 'Cause love

CODA
E♭   Kids: E♭6/B♭   E♭maj7   E♭6/B♭   ADULT: B♭9sus

up! (La la la la la la la) True love just nev-er gives

E♭ Kids: E♭6/B♭   E♭maj7   E♭6/B♭   ALL: B♭9sus   E♭

up! (La la la la la la la) True love just nev-er gives up!

8va

MY FATHER'S angels

words by William J.
and Gloria Gaither

music by Dony McGuire

Slow 4, gentle feel

KIDS:

They're all a-

bove me, _____ be - neath me, _____ be - fore me, _____ they're all a-round me — My Fa-ther's an - gels all pro - tect me ev-'ry -

where._____

1. They're all a -

2,3.

VERSE

(*opt.* SOLO) 1. I could nev - er stray_ so far_ my Fa - ther_____would lose track_

(KIDS) 2. E - ven when_the night's_ so dark_ I just can't see a

_____ of where I am;_____ An - gels walk_ be - side_ me, hold - ing tight -

thing in front of me, I won't need_ to wor - ry - they can see,_

2nd time to coda

84

- ly _____ to my hand. They're all a-

D.S. to chorus
D.S. to chorus

CODA

they see me! _____ They're all a-bove me, _____ be-

neath me, _____ be-fore me, _____ they're all a-round me— My Fa-ther's

an-gels all pro-tect me, My Fa-ther's an-gels all pro-tect me, My Fa-ther's an - gels all pro - tect me.

They're all a - bove me,_____ be - neath me,_____ be -

fore me,_____ they're all a - round me — My Fa-ther's an - gels all pro -

tect me ev - 'ry - where._____

Sing WITH US (MEDLEY)

Jesus Loves The Little Children

Je - sus loves the lit - tle chil - dren, all the chil - dren of the

world! Red and yel - low, black and white, they are

pre - cious in His sight, Je - sus loves the lit - tle chil - dren of the world!

2.

world! Je - sus loves the lit - tle chil - dren _____ "That means all the children!" of the

rit. *slower*

I'd Like To Teach The World To Sing

Words and Music by Roger Cook, Billy Davis,
Bill Backer, and Roger Greenaway

Brightly

world! I'd

like to teach the world to sing __ in per - fect har - mo - ny, __

88

a song of love ___ that ech - oes on ___ and

1.

C   G

nev - er goes ___ a - way ___

2.

C *sub. rit.*   G

I'd nev - er goes a - way

sub. rit.

Only A Boy Named David

C

Bright two-beat

"Here's a song about a boy in the Bible, named David. Hey, I think you'll like him!"

Bright two-beat

F   C9

F

On - ly a boy named Dav - id,   He had on - ly a   lit - tle

C7
F
sling. On - ly a boy named Da - vid, but
G7
C7
F
he could pray and sing. On - ly a boy named
F7
B♭
Da - vid, On - ly a rip - pling brook.
3
F
On - ly a boy named Da - vid, but

five _____ lit - tle stones he took, and

one lit - tle stone went in the sling, and the sling went 'round and

'round, and one lit - tle stone went in the sling, and the

sling went 'round and 'round! And _____ 'round and 'round and 'round and 'round and 'round and 'round and 'round and

one lit - tle stone went up in the air, *(penny whistle)* _____

1.

and the giant came tumb - ling

down!

Shadrach, Meshach, Abednego

Words and Music by Hugh Mitchell

Moderate 4

"Here's three guys who really knew what they believed!"

Three good men lived

Lyrics:

ve - ry long a - go: Shad - rach, Me - shach,

and A - bed - ne - go. To an i - dol

they would nev - er bow; Shad - rach, Me - shach, and A - bed - ne - go.

In - to a fie - ry fur - nace they were there-fore cast; Neb - u - chad-nez - zar thought they'd

C7 F

never last! But God was there, He never let them go!

C7 F C7 F Bb/C

Shadrach, Meshach, and Abednego! Shad-rach!

F/C C7 F C7 F

Meshach! and Abednego!

All Night, All Day

G Gently

A D/A Amaj7 D/A A D/A Amaj7 D/A

p ——— ——— *p sim.*

All night, all _____ day, An - gels watch-in' o - ver me, my Lord!__ All night, all _____ day,

an - gels watch-in' o - ver me! All night,

all _____ day, An - gels watch-in' o - ver me!

Safe Am I

Words and Music by Mildred Dillon

An - gels watch - in' o - ver me! Safe am

H

I, safe am I, in the hol - low of His

hand; Shel - tered o'er, shel - tered o'er in His

love for - ev - er - more. No ill can

harm me, no foe a-larm me, for He keeps both day and night. Safe am I, safe am I, in the hol-low of His hand! No ill can hand!

God Is Watching Over You
Words and Music by Rick Powell

Slowly-rubato

God is watch-ing o-ver you, watch-ing o-ver you,

watch-ing o-ver you. God is watch-ing o-ver you,

1.
watch-ing o-ver you to-day.

2.
watch-ing o-ver you

"Today, tonight, tomorrow and forever..."

TELL IT TO A *Few* CLOSE FRIENDS

Words by Gloria Gaither

Music by William J. Gaither

Moderate 2

Verse

1) You say you could do more if you just had tal-ent, and were
you'd be ter-rif-ic if you just could tra-vel, and you
(2) read - y to set the world on fire___ just as
wor - ry a - bout the ques-tions and prob-lems— let the

giv - en a place___ to be - gin,___ A place to tell___ all the
had a lot of mon-ey to spend;___ You wish that you___ were a
soon as your ship___ comes in!___ Why don't you get your___
Spir - it show you where and when.___ Re - lax___ and let

world a - bout Je - sus. Well, tell it to a few close friends.. And
nat - u - ral lead - er. Well, tell it to a few close friends.. Don't
act to - geth - er, And tell it to a few close friends?
love do the talk - ing, And start with just a few close friends..

Chorus

You can tell it, tell it right where you're liv - ing—you've got

Je - sus to rec - om - mend.__ You can tell it to the

world at your door - step—Just tell it to a few close friends.__ 2) You're

2nd time to Coda ⊕   D.S. al Coda

⊕ CODA   Fine

THAT'S Him

Words by Joy MacKenzie

Music by Rick Powell

Lightly (♩ = 132)

Is - n't it just like Him to want to walk with us, Just the kind of friend He is to want to laugh and talk with us;

Lis-t'ning to the things we say and join-ing in the games we play, Shar - ing, car - ing, that's His way!

Just like a fa-ther un-der-stands his own, Knows what it's like to be a-fraid or lost or all a-lone;

He is up a-bove to watch and heal and help and love you, That's Him! That's Him!

You can be

short, fat, red-haired and freck-le faced, Dressed in a shirt with big holes and your shoes un-laced;

Tall, thin, with red, black or yel-low skin, Still He loves you, that's just Him! He likes

blue-jeans, jel-ly beans, hot dogs and bub-ble gum, He does-n't care what your name is or where you're from

Just call on Him and He'll be there to help you al-ways, that's Him! That's Him!

Just call on Him and He'll be there to help you al-ways that's Him! That's Him!

THE Monster SONG

words by Joy MacKenzie   music by Bill George

Moderately, fast 2 ("spooky"!)

CHORUS
KIDS:

If for just a mo-ment you for-get what you're a-bout, And o-pen up that door a crack there's hard-ly an-y doubt: The mon-sters 'll get ya- you bet-ter watch out! The

mon-sters 'll get ya——— you bet-ter watch— out!

3rd time to coda ✛ G♯7 A7

3rd time to coda ✛

VERSE

*(SOLO) 1. GRIZ - ZLY GREED with his grab - by claws
(SOLO) 2. High in the cor - ner, way out of the light is a

*Each "monster" (i.e. greed, jealousy) may be represented by individual solo voices.

Dm
A
A7
Dm
snatch - es what he catch - es for his juic - y jaws; And
nest of wid - ow spi - ders—some black, some white:
G♯o
JAD - ED OLD JEAL - OUS - Y comes creep - in' 'cross the floor to
LIES, they are, who spin a web so taut that the
Gm6
A7
make you hate what you loved be - fore!
tin - i - est of them will get you hope - less - ly caught!
Dm
B♭
Gm
A
mf
AR - RO - GRANT E - GO with his cap - i - tal "I's"
DAN - GER! DIS - HON - EST - Y! - He'll hyp - no - tize your mind, make the
mf

leers from be - hind his hum - ble dis - guise While
bad look good, the cru - el kind; He

OLD TY - RANT TEM - PER lurks be - hind your back and
bribes be - hav - ior with temp - ta - tions sweet - then he's

watch- es his chance for a sneak at - tack!_____
got ya: get a mir - ror, take a look at a cheat!_____

Repeat twice to chorus
Repeat twice chorus

CODA
(KIDS continue)
A7

CODA
It's when you least ex - pect it that you be -

108

no one else to blame! So roll the great hu-

mon - gous stone in - to the door of the cave, and

block it for - ev - er! Don't pre-tend to be

brave, But arm your - self with the truth

110

A7
Dm
geth - er we can trap them so there's not a sin - gle doubt- The
C♯o
Dm
C♯o
mon- sters can't get ya - ha! ha! ha! The
Gm
A7
Dm
mon-sters can't get ya: they'll nev - er get out!
G♯o
A
Dm
G♯o
A
G♯o
Dm
A7
Dm
f

THIS IS THE DAY THE LORD HAS MADE

Words by William J. and Gloria Gaither

Music by William J. Gaither

1. Make a joyful noise unto the Lord, all ye lands! Serve the Lord with gladness;
2. We are His people and the sheep of His pastures. Enter into His gates with thanksgiving; come into

(1.) Come before His presence with singing.
(2.) His courts with praise. Be thankful to Him, and

Know ye that the Lord, He is God. It is He that hath made us, and not we ourselves.

bless His name. For the Lord is good, His mercy is everlasting, His truth endureth to all generations!

C
This is the day that the Lord has made
Let us re - joice and be glad
C7
F
This is the day that the Lord has made
Let us re - joice and be glad
C
G
C
This is the day that the
F
C
Lord has made
C
second time to Coda
Let us re - joice and be glad

He gave us to-day, ____ so give Him our praise, re-joice and be glad! _____ The mea-dows and hills__ are re-joic -ing__ (spoken)The flow-ers and trees__ clap their hands! The moun-tains break forth in-to sing -ing__ The

F F♯dim C/G G7 C
praise of our Lord fills the land. The joy and the laugh - ter of
F C
chil - dren join the praise of the a - ged and wise.
F F♯dim C/G F♯dim C/G
Je - sus is king! Come join and sing
G C F/G
D.S. al Coda
praise from the sky!
3

Now I can see ____ He cares a-bout me ____ Come on and

sing _____ *Je - sus is king!* Let's live our days

Hearts full of praise ____ re - joice and be glad _____

____ re - joice and be glad! _____

You're SOMETHING SPECIAL

Words by William J. and Gloria Gaither

Music by William J. Gaither

1. When Je - sus sent you to us, we loved you from the start; You were
have a lit - tle sis - ter who's not at all like me; She can
dad - dy mows the back-yard, my mom - my makes the bed; My

just a bit of sun - shine from heav - en to our hearts. Not
write a love - ly poem but I can climb a tree. My
bro - ther cleans his play - room, I see the dog gets fed. And

just an - oth - er ba - by 'cause since the world be - gan, There's been
bro - ther too is dif - f'rent with freck - les on his nose, When my
each one needs the oth - er to help him thro' the day, And

118

some-thing ver-y spec-ial for you in His plan. That's why
ques-tions need_ an-swers, he's the one who knows. That's why
love must be the rea-son God planned it that way. That's why

CHORUS

He made you spec-ial, you're the on-ly one of your kind, God
I'm some-thing spec-ial, I'm the on-ly one of my kind, God
He made me spec-ial, I'm the on-ly one of my kind, God

gave you a bod-y and a bright health-y mind; He
gave me a bod-y and a bright health-y mind; He
gave me a bod-y and a bright health-y mind; He

had a spec-ial pur-pose that He want-ed you to find, so He
had a spec-ial pur-pose that He want-ed me to find, so He
had a spec-ial pur-pose that He want-ed me to find, so He

made you some-thing spec-ial, you're the on - ly one of your
made me some-thing spec-ial, I'm the on - ly one of my
made me some-thing spec-ial, I'm the on - ly one of my
1.2.
3.
To Next Strain
kind. 2. I
kind. 3. My
kind, He made you some-thing
spec - ial, He made you some-thing spec-ial, you're the
on - ly one of your kind.

index